*Thoughts
that come
to mind*

Thoughts that come to mind

POEMS TO HEAL AND NURTURE THE SOUL

Annie Moore

First published in 2021 by Moorwellbeing
www.moorwellbeing.com

Copyright © 2021 Annie Moore

Illustrations by Catherine Hennessy
Book design by Annette Peppis
Cover photography by Annie Moore
Consultation: Tony Mulliken
Printed by Ingram Sparks

ISBN 978-1-3999-0357-8

I would like to dedicate this book to my son Tom who died in 2014 at the age of 34 of a terrible blood cancer – acute myeloid leukaemia, that simply took our breath away.

Also, to my family who have experienced the never ending deep dark hole with me. Terry, Hollie, Katie and son, Archie have shown enormous courage and resilience in the years since Tom passed.

It is because of their strength and support that together we have been able to continue building a new life around the old and in the middle of this enigma have treasured Tom's memories, sharing them with Archie, wrapped in love, laughter and joy.

Contents

CHAPTER 1 **Nature thoughts**   11

Grasses   13
Dew Drop   15
The Beach   17
Surf   19
Golden Hour   21
Blowing   23
Sun   25
Ancao   27
Sea   29
Barril   31
Pebbles   33
Earthlight   35
Snowfall   37
Wind   39
Mist   41

CHAPTER 2 **Nurturing thoughts**   43

Gentle Man   45
Best Boy   47
Being Me   49
Marriage   50
No Doubt   53
Change   55
Young Heart   57
Woman   59

CHAPTER 3 **Healing thoughts**   61

Acceptance   63
Cycle of Life   64
Flourish   67
Joy   69
Thanks   71
Comfort   73
Resting   75
In the Moment   76
Flow and Grow   78
This Place   81
Sounds   82
Blessings   85
Seeds of Change   86
Tree of Hope   89
Breathe In   91
Universe   93
Gratitude   95
Let It Go   97
Freedom   99
Ego   101
Contemplation   103
Peace   105
Senses   107
Truth   109
Love   111

CHAPTER 4 Mother thoughts   113

Influencer   115
Hidden   117
Elements   119
My Soul Sings   121
Sense of Knowing   123
Awareness   125
Moon Whispers   127
Stillness   129
Field of Hope   131
Which Way   133
Standing Strong   135
Woman Goddess   137
Sound In Me   139
Unplug   141
Heroine   143
Mother Thoughts   145
Resting   147
My View   149

A Gift for You   150
Moon to Heart Meditation   151

About the author   153
Thank you   154

CHAPTER 1

Nature thoughts

"Detach from thought, accept the sounds,
surrender to the ground."

Grasses

When the wind blows
grasses will flow
like dancing creatures
high and low.

When the wind blows
our senses are heightened
listening, tuning
into a distant crow.

When the wind blows
we are alert,
alive, aware
that our mind and body
are merely here to grow.

When the wind blows
we feel at one with the earth
connected to the outside air,
nature and our inner soul.

Dew Drop

Sitting here feeling the breeze tickle my face,
the dense dew at my feet,
the damp mist in the air.

I feel a sense of mystery an evolving stillness
that is emotionless,
timeless and oh so rare.

The magic of the silvery sky is breath-taking,
comforting wrapping
its cover, around me.

Here I hold the power within
to influence all magnificence
opening my heart to let go and be free.

In the calmness of my mind, I know
the fog will disperse bringing more clarity
lifting the morning light.

Reveal yourself misty maker move into the warmth
of my soul for there is a shining light within us all
waiting to break through whatever day or night.

The Beach

The beach is bare
there is no one there.
The sand is fair
with no one to share.

Alone on the beach
except for you.
My darling boy once here
but now so far away.

Drifting in and out of loneliness
I find solace in your memory
strong and vibrant in my heart.

The beach is where we come together,
you, me, sand and sea
there is no other place I'd rather be.

Surf

The surf is high
the surf is low
crashing and tumbling to and fro.

The surfer is crouching
the surfer is cool
riding the waves with precision and fuel.

The woman is standing
the woman is alone
jumping and diving in the break.

She leaps and prances
under and over rolling
in the waves like a ferocious dancer.

She is strong
she is powerful
glimmering in the foam.

She is the light
she has the right
to be at one with the sea.

Golden Hour

There is a light of warmth in sight
first in the morning light
and last eve of night.

The golden yellow sunlight reflects
its fiery hues with deep intensity
covering and claiming its surroundings.

The force is warm
the essence is dreamy
illuminating everything in view.

For this is the golden hour
of beauty and bliss
best part of the day never to miss.

Blowing

How the wind blows strong and fierce
building to a crescendo across the valley.

Gigantic palm leaves shout and
clatter their arms in distress.

The sail hanging over the deck
waves and rocks, pulling on the
fastenings attached.

There is movement from the sturdy poles
rooted in the ground, safe and secure
without making a sound.

With each roar and climax of wind
I lift my head to acknowledge the gust.

The garden sprinklers spray and play
with my face, feeling cool
and wet against my skin.

There is energy in the air driving me on
I know now not to wonder
at the power of this turbulent force.

Its capacity growing stronger with every breath
bringing me deeper towards an
awareness of inner rest.

Sun

The sun rises, the sun sets
the sun shines through a misty mess.

The sun gives off warmth through
the day and into the night.

The uplifting intensity penetrates
Into the earth with all its might.

The energy we absorb enlightens our soul
the power we receive is stronger
than anything else we know.

The sun is our saviour, our guide,
our source, with all that we love
shrouded in its glory and spiritual force.

Ancao

On Ancao beach I hear the sounds of the sea
bound together in unison
crashing waves, tumbling white foam
echoing along the shore.

Slow rhythmical movement of deep aqua blue
casts dark shadows across the bay
waiting to be stirred and provoked.

Above the surface the taste of fresh salty air
lingers like vinegar over salted fish and chips.

Leaving the sea, I walk along the flat wet shore
making footprints like never before.

Slowly pacing onto the soft golden sand
endlessly scorched by the sun.
I sit and observe.

No one is here just yet to interrupt
the peace and calm overpowering
even the wildest noises form the sea.

So NOW that I dwell on this wonderful moment
while mesmerised by unceasing hypnotic sounds
I find stillness within to stop,
listen and feel at one with my soul.

Sea

Praise to the sea for being
powerful
positive
petulant and free.

Woe to the sea for bringing
bountiful
beauty
and belligerence to me.

Celebrate our sea for
energy
expression
and eternity for all to see.

Thankful to the sea for evoking
calm
control
and centred aura from
our inner most seal.

Barril

Glimpse across the sand
over the wash of the waves
going deeper into the distance
of the deep navy sea.

Let your eyes rest a while on the horizon
focusing on the perfectly fine line
drawn around the world.

As your gaze continues up into the perfect
clear sky, one wonders
"wouldn't it be nice to be here all the time".

Pebbles

A pocket of pebbles
is filled with random dreams.

Thoughts drift in and drift out
synchronising with the gentle breeze.

Being mesmerised by the smooth
surface massaging my fingertips.

I am immersed here for a moment
while life stands still.

Soothing and peaceful with no
pressure to be anything other
than who I am at will.

Earthlight

The sky is grey
the earth is brown
the clouds hang heavy
weighted down.

The wind gusts in a flurry
while I kneel and pray
sending love to all
who may be longing,
to be free.

Snowfall

Snow falling, like a moving wall
floating down from above
rhythmical, mesmerising, magical
before my eyes.

Falling, festooning, filling
a moment in my mind
thickening, transporting, tainting
every surface where it lands.

There is much to contemplate,
pure, plentiful, playful
changing the landscape from
dreary to a dazzling sight.

No sounds, no scent, no sensation
is evidence of calm framing
an aptitude of stillness
magnificent in a potency of white.

Wind

The wind is strong
coming and going
in blasts and flurries
warm and refreshing.

The sun beats down
piercing the ground
with fire and force
to awaken and alert.

The wind carries the clouds
across the crazy blue sky
gently caressing the branches
swaying in the breeze.

The sail blows gracefully
up and down
I feel relaxed with the
rhythm that connects
with what I have found.

Mist

Before I begin, I observe the
early morning mist covering the valley
hovering over the fields and trees.

At the end I open my eyes
the mist has cleared moving
from the valley to the top of the hills
hanging like a sheet of dust
skimming the horizon.

So much splendour rests before my eyes
so much wonder to feel behind my closed eyes
so spectacular to see this vision within my third eye.

CHAPTER 2

Nurturing thoughts

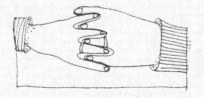

"Flowing from outside, growing
from inside."

Gentle Man

My heart is full of forgiveness
my heart is full of grief
my heart is full of warmth
for I know not where to go.

My heart is leading me upwards
towards the highest mountain above
my heart brings me into a moment
of peace and love.

My heart is full of wonder
my heart is heavy with sorrow
my heart is bursting with memories
reminding me of you.

My heart is full, my eyes are full
but most of all I feel blessed to
have been full of you.

Best Boy

Skipping across the sand
running by the shore
his shadow against the sea
looking up to the dark pink-orange sky.

Now he is in front of me
sprinting fast and free
grinning and laughing
in a wondrous moment of glee.

Being Me

Do we think we are breaking new ground
with thoughts and delusions
that satisfy the crowd.

This is not what we are here for
this is not what we see
this is not our true sense of destiny.

We have longing love and laughter
in our bones waiting like
a child to be set free.

Our life is full of pressure to
perform, preen and be seen
but what if we stop, take a breath,
look inside at what we could be.

With passion to follow our dreams
power to overcome our limited beliefs
practice to master our wondering thoughts
pleasure to influence those who have yet to be taught.

These are the thoughts of a wondering me
ready to reach out in a world full of misery
and invite you into a sea of love and fantasy
where you may rest and discover how to just BE.

Marriage

A marriage in heaven
is a marriage with you
husband and wife
it just takes two.

A partnership together
is a pledge for life
as you and I both
embrace love and strife.

We have our differences
we have our woes
we trust each other
as our deepest love grows.

We are a team
we are soul mates
we are lovers
knitted together like a seam.

We dance and play in our magical way
claiming happiness, joy and peace
feeling at one with each other
as we open our hearts and say.

'You are my rock
of safety and comfort
you give me strength
to conquer with passion.'

No one can take us away
from our special place
of bountiful grace
filling our every day.

Love is the foundation
of this beautiful partnership
joining our hearts and feelings
in a harmony of loving kinship.

No Doubt

This is the moment
now is the time
they have arrived
in this place of harmony.

There were moments of doubt
harsh reminders
of torment and sadness
not knowing which way to go.

Deep down the path was clear
be it unsure at the time
waiting and longing faded away
as hunger and joy burst through.

No doubt now whatever may
come between them
will be crushed and broken by
the mighty force of true love.

Change

The change in me is the change in you
a slow progression of mistakes and fears
measured by the turbulence
of the outside world.

Along my journey
of doubts and misgivings
I have longed to be the perfect me.

Perfection is not what it seems
there is no freedom in flawlessness
no joy in smugness.

Exactness can restrict the beauty of song
echoed in the swaying trees
and mountains beyond.

I am no longer tied to my inborn belief
I am free to express myself in any degree
for I know that my essence is the essential part of me.

I am the change I see in you and me.

Young Heart

Listen to your heart
visit your plentiful place
hold the love within you.

Listen to your inner wisdom
open your spirit centre
celebrate your passion and pleasure
embrace the nature that surrounds you.

Listen to your inner self
feel the growth deep within
hold the space where
breath meets stillness
pause and be yourself.

Listen to your soul
sense the love and
empathy unfolding
blessed beautiful
deserving to exist.

Woman

She is a ray of sunshine on a cloudy day

She smiles even when she's sad

She laughs and cries too

She is stronger than anyone realises

She never gives up

She knows that life is precious

She lives with hope in her lap

She is like the sea, mesmerising to watch

She would do anything to protect her loved ones

She is woman to you.

CHAPTER 3

Healing thoughts

"To be in the nothing is to be
at one with yourself."

Acceptance

Today I accept myself as I truly am
a being of love, passion and peace.

I can see my faults and bad habits
falling away into a vessel of forgiveness.

Aware of shock and trauma
bouncing off solid walls
no longer penetrating the resilience
that has grown inside.

I realise there is space to look back
at achievements through my life
wrapping my arms around them
to acknowledge endurance of toil and strife.

Always the driving force pushing
from within to restore faith and hope
I know I have the magnificent ability
to live a life, I love.

Cycle of Life

We evolve through a cyclical cycle
like beings passing in the night.

We are a hotel for our spirit light
to shine from birth and beyond.

Taking care of our dreams and desires
 as we grow and mature like ripened fruit.

While nurturing our habitat we clean and provide,
rear and hide within walls of secrets and pride.

Ours is a castle full of happiness and joy
where our children flourish and develop
absorbing life's knocks and falls.

It is within these four walls after our children
have flown that we contemplate our purpose.

Consciously making decisions about
what we are here to do.

There is a yearning inside to do our life's work
experience a sense of inner peace.

Mindfully acknowledging that what we have
learned is within our conscious belief.

There is truth, fulfilment, realisation
of who we really are.

Appreciation of the cyclical flow
from birth to death freeing our
physical form from pain and distress.

We know we will return to spirit
resting in another sphere,
satisfied that we have cared for
our home within our soul.

Flourish

Now is the time to flourish and grow.

I have observed, learnt and delivered
over the years care and control.

There have been hurdles and burdens to overcome
messages and Angels to help and support.

Amongst the confusion, worry and sorrow
the universe has pointed the way.

To forgive, be grateful, show love
and compassion to those along the way.

Thank you, Angels for shining your light
to lead me on a soulful path of inner sight.

Joy

Joy to the world
Joy to the people
Joy in the spirit that is part of you.

Joy in your name
Joy in your frame
Joy in your being a better person.

Joy in your love
Joy in your heart
Joy in the blessings that are sent from above.

Joy from the earth
Joy from the universe
Joy from the heavens in every verse.

We are joy, you are joy, they are joy
I am full of joy on this joyful day.

Thanks

Being alive and well is a blessing from above
seeing the bright yellow sun
and deep blue sky shine their love.

We look, we see, we feel, we think
with our hearts as one savouring each moment
that comes and goes in a blink.

Deep inside we are fragile, sensitive and kind
waiting to be heard by those in the
distance who have been unkind.

Where are we going without thanks in our thoughts
no one will bless us or forgive our remorse.

So summon your energy deep from within
to tell all who you see how grateful you have been.

Comfort

In the silence I become
aware of the stillness
observe the feeling.

Detach from thoughts
accept the sounds
surrender to the ground.

Finding the pause brings clarity
while resting delivers
peace simply withdrawing
awakens my soul.

Nestling in contemplation
I feel at home
knowing of happiness in my space
freedom in the refuge
of my comfort place.

Resting

Resting in my outside world
I am attuned
into the area that surrounds me.

Moving from one to the other
like a gentle breeze
I hear the distant humming of the bees.

Stillness lingers while fresh smells
of the countryside permeate the air
Cockerels crowing, goats bleating
are welcome music to my ears.

I bathe in nature's influence
to ground my thoughts
of what I see before me
is beauty everywhere.

Bringing distant pleasures together
from land and sea coherently
I stay living quietly in a corner
of nature inside eternity.

In the Moment

Tuning into my breath I feel blessed
with peace and tranquillity.

Listening to sounds of water
trickling away in the orange light
I am transported into the echo of a
waterfall cascading with huge capacity.

Sparkling droplets caress the rocks
touch the leaves dancing
and dripping in the breeze.

There is so much we can cherish
in our mind while in a
moment ready to unwind.

Open your eyes and ears
to all that nature gives
encounter your thoughts
drifting into heavenly bliss.

This is the instance
we are learning to accept
whatever passes through
has our deepest respect.

Our moment is centred
powerful and free
with no burden of thought
to interrupt calm serenity.

Flow and Grow

As we grow,
we naturally flow
with life
allowing our
inner soul
to expand
with ease.

We are calm
in stillness
passionate in motion
strong in silence
peaceful in thought.

Flowing effortlessly
with gravity
and calm
not a sound
we make.

Here we embrace
our inner most
natural state
with fluidity
and grace.

Our motion akin
to restful
quiet owning
the rhythm
of yin.

This Place

I love where I am
I love what I see
I love that I come here
feeling lovingly free.

When I am low
when I am lost
when I need comfort
it comes with a cost.

In and out
weaving and wanting
through a mesh
of feelings that
I need to let go.

Testing my ability
to sit
just be
in the process
of embracing
my spirituality.

Sounds

Sounds are powerful
sounds evoke love
infuse tension
gather momentum
amplify conscious awareness.

Sounds muster intention
induce vibration
send messages into our world
mimicking a multitude of feelings
from somewhere deep inside.

Sounds make us happy
bathed in enigma
sounds make us sad
doing battle with
the noise in our head.

Sounds are wanting
deep down drowned
by the pressure of
what we believe is
going on all around.

We are the result of sounds
waiting to be heard
rising, awakening
within our groin.

These are the sounds
we fear the most
in the silence of our
commanding restless
thoughts.

Blessings

You are blessed today
ageless, radiant, and able.

All day, every day and forever more
you command this earth
that allows you to breathe.

There is turmoil
there is sorrow,
suffering and fear.

There is transformation
bringing the change
you wish to see.

Gratitude, forgiveness,
compassion and devotion
consciously alter your world
with a mystical measure of one degree.

Seeds of Change

Transition leads to change
whether small or big
transformation will evolve
in all corners of life
change is inevitable.

There is much to take hold of
plenty to let go of
as new beginnings arise
from seeds planted in good faith.

I awaken to discover
the prospects presented
significant, tormenting
and forthcoming.

I am conscious of the shift
sometimes moving quickly
often very slowly
depending on my mood.

I acknowledge life is short
desperate for time
the deeper I dwell
the stronger my choices.

While suffering is always there
lurking in the cracks
here is my chance
to welcome the energy
of the seeds of change.

Tree of Hope

Standing tall and bleak
oozing resilience
against all odds
no longer with branches,
leaves, flowers or fruit.

Standing still, strong and firm
in a space of acceptance
without judgement
day in day out.

No fears, no doubts,
no ambiguity
unaffected by anything
going on around
strong presence speaks to me
from power in the tree of hope.

Breathe In

Breathe in new life
Breathe out letting go.

Breathe in the moment
Breathe out acceptance.

Breathe in fresh air
Breathe out release.

Breathe in energy
Breathe out relax.

Breathe in joy
Breathe out forgiveness.

Breathe in love
Breathe out happiness.

Breathe in peace
Breathe out freedom.

Universe

I trust my mind and body
I trust my heart and soul
I trust the universe
to show me the way.

I trust myself implicitly
I trust myself in the moment
I trust what I have is what I need
I trust nothing more, nothing less.

I trust I am enough.

Gratitude

Gratitude blocks envy
Gratitude blocks resentment
Gratitude blocks regret.

Gratitude turns what we have
into enough
Gratitude is the greatest gift
Gratitude brings us joy.

Gratitude does not ask
for anything in return
Gratitude has no fear.

Gratitude is good
Gratitude is plentiful
Gratitude is love
and much more.

Let It Go

Let it flow, let it go
through thoughts of peace
and equanimity.

Let it flow, let it go
into the breath filling your
body with wisdom and joy.

Let it flow, let it go
moving and dancing
with wondrous strength and vitality.

Let it flow, let it go
into the realms of divinity
nurturing those who surround you.

Let it flow, let it go
for you are the creator
of your own destiny.

Freedom

When I feel happy
I feel hurt.

With suffering comes sadness
with happiness comes joy.

The seed of anguish may be strong
the seed of love is more prolonged.

Letting go gives us freedom
the one and only rider of happiness.

In our hearts we cling
to anything that will set us free.

We hide from the life
of discomfort of all that we see.

Ego

Ego in me
sees the ego in you.
Ego is driving behaviour
takes over during catastrophe.

Behind the ego lurks fear
behind the ego there is much to reveal
behind the ego lies turmoil and grief.

Step back from the ego
step from the mind into the heart
step out of yourself, let go.

Move away from the ego of
always wanting to be right
move beyond the ego
step into the light.

Contemplation

Now is the moment
in one single pause
to dwell in the present.

Now is to create
in a breath
taste the freshness
hear birds boldly singing.

Now is to feel warmth
of the gentle breeze
smell the heat of nature.

Now is to have time
to contemplate
time to just be.

Peace

Today I make peace
with myself and
the ones I love.

Today I stand my ground.

Today I have strength
to hold peace in my heart
moving beyond anxieties
I breathe.

Today I stand my ground.

Today I have a voice
I am not afraid
of the differences we have
within our lives.

Today I stand my ground.

Today I am stepping back
letting go of any resistance
with compassion
I know how to say no.

Senses

Simple stillness
soaks the senses

Sounds of cars, birds
and barking dogs.

Smells of sweetness emerge
from flowers and shrubs.

Touching the magic
of delicate grasses under my feet.

Tasting the meaningfulness
of the morning air.

Wrapping my arms around these senses
stimulates every cell that rises within.

I nurture, arouse and empower
this moment to withdraw
hailing the light therein.

Truth

Speak with honesty
shine the light of integrity
in your heart.

Speak with awareness
of those who are listening
to all you say.

Speak with compassion,
knowledge and bring kindness
into play.

Speak with graceful respect
never without thought for others
following your path.

Speak with love, forgiveness
and gratitude for these are the truths
created to last.

Love

Love is perfection
of the highest degree
to love and be loved makes
one boundlessly free

Knowing love is what
we all need to see
to accept love can be
hard to agree.

Being loved is
the best it can be
to feel love is
empowering for me.

True love is the ultimate
level of ecstasy
make time to love
and you will see.

CHAPTER 4

Mother thoughts

"Be who you are,
not who you think you are."

Influencer

Dear Mother Earth
your strength is my resolve
your wisdom my resilience
your nurture my desire
your power is deep within my heart.

All that you embrace I contemplate
showing me the way to freedom
that I thought was lost.

You bring happiness and joy to every
encounter I behold
without you I am nothing
with you I am magnificent.

Let us be one together in life
and for ever more.

Hidden

Deep inside hidden from the world
an inner sanctuary exists
calling, listening, whispering
untold myths

Ancient, precious, magical mysteries remain
waiting to be revealed like a
wondrous shining cloak
opening wide to display sparkling
effervescent elements of inspiration and joy.

Speaking to our soul with love and purpose
we step inside for a moment to rest,
embracing the feeling of lightness
floating in weightless harmony
while waiting to ignite our conscious intent.

This is the everlasting peace we strive for
with longing and hope at its core
never battling or forcing
simply resting and waiting to behold
with patience and love on side.

For here is the dream
the reality and the glory
of our hidden seam.

Elements

Resting in awareness
rising in motion
is part of the journey
you embrace through transformation.

You are at one with the elements
as you explore all that you touch
with warmth and devotion.

The air dances around the trees
lightly brushing your skin.

The earth beneath your feet
brings protection with strength
and abundance.

Water flowing through emotions
drinks the energy from
your womb space.

All that you need is being replenished
at source through the
empowering essence of
wisdom, vitality and bliss.

My Soul Sings

My soul sings with delight
my soul dances in the moonlight
my soul listens to my prayers
my soul drinks in the fresh air.

My soul is waiting to kindle
the power from within
driving the energy of youth
into every single cell.

My soul is the essence of being
awakening all that I have
all that I will ever need.

My soul is the shining light
that rises up to protect, love
and guide me in everything I do.

My soul sings out to you and into me.

Sense Of Knowing

Knowing the smell of the sea
is to breathe salt into the skin
replenishing, healing the way.

Its pure freshness of life force
nourishes every part of me
with knowing contentment
as if to say 'I love you back.'

Trusting the sea to melt into
the horizon will draw
it deeper towards immensity
while standing strong
its dazzling blue coat
fades into the endless sky.

There is peace in the knowing
that when two forces meet
they melt into infinity.

Awareness

Awareness sinks deep into the earth
penetrating slowly
extending, anchoring,
securing.

Forming a foundation
driving inwardly
enhancing any motive
to build and flourish.

Open the gateway
peel off the signs
that prevent you from
moving forward.

Take a leap
take a chance
let your courage
feed the intention
to enter the kingdom of peace.

Moon Whispers

Moon whispers in the dark
sending messages to my heart

lingering around the time
when the womb space is alight.

Soft and open to receive
with radiance and beauty

awakening during her cycle
to become connected to
Earth, fire and life

She evolves, swells and
penetrates our feminine dreams.

Magical rhythms move with
inner most desires
seeking the presence of tenderness
abundance and love.

Stillness

Where is stillness in the moment
where is stillness in the breath
where is stillness in the body
where is stillness on earth?

There is stillness in the quiet
there is stillness in the air around
there is stillness in a body free of tension
there is stillness in the slow rhythm of the breath.

Stillness is in silence
stillness slows the mind
stillness comforts the heart
stillness settles the unconscious.

When we rest in stillness
we are connected,
conscious and
content.

Field of Hope

A sense of hope deepens
as awareness evolves

through a mind filled with fog
distant and forgetful

now emerging into a field of hope
where a sea of lotus flowers come to rest

opening with radiant grace
mesmerising in the sway of the breeze.

There is much to empower
in the awareness of hope

making room for beauty and strength
to overwhelmingly succeed.

Which Way

Breathing in freshness of life brings
nourishment, richness, refreshing the parts.

Finding peace in the breath
is to recognise where our forces meet.

Strong, powerful and magnificent
each breath we take softens our state.

While melting and mounting with a flicker of magic
the breath shows us the way.

Standing Strong

A presence of strength
builds a firm foundation

powerfully rooting into the ground
with firmness that speaks of safety.

Beckoning to master stability with ease
her warrior force is potent in spirit

reaching to find refuge in the warmth
of a womb that is vital, feminine and free.

There to recognise the power of strength
will live forever within the empowerment
of love through to eternity

Woman Goddess

She carries the divine feminine of life
diving down into her goddess energy
dark and feisty.

Exploring what it means to be a woman
rising and falling with the seasons of time.

She yearns to ignite her creative spirit
flowing through rhythms and cycles
that change as she grows.

Born out of gentle touch she heals
her mother daughter wounds
facing fears with calm and control.

She is blessed by her wisdom years
connecting with her internal journey
wrapping herself in comfort and love.

She is the maker, the mourner,
the mother of life
who emerges into her second spring
in a powerful, commanding light.

Sound in Me

Sounds from the sea
sounds from the wind
sounds from the trees
sounds unto Me.

Awakening forces in the sea
awakening voices in the wind
awakening spirit in the trees
awakening energy in Me.

Rising like a serpent
powerfully untamed
acknowledging with love
how much it means to Me.

Unplug

I watch the breath
observe the quiet
connect to a slow gentle rhythm.

Notice mindful presence
in body and mind
waterfalls of thoughts
come and go
emotions flow in trickling drops.

Anxiety and troubles melt away
regressing with experience
of conscious reaction
to the clearing of thoughts
heavily lifted by an almighty hand

There to unplug from daily strife
settle and soften in the nothing
of directing intent
being in the now
with the sound of silence.

Heroine

How does she look
how does she feel
when her demons
are beseeching her.

How does she act
how does she answer
to the call of her
feminine devotee.

How is her spirit
how is her energy
waiting to awaken
and set her free.

How does she emerge
how does she blossom
amid her
internal enquiry.

She waits
she listens
to the call of her
sorcerer releasing her
soul from captivity.

Mother Thoughts

I recall my thoughts
I know I'm breathing in
I know I'm breathing out.

My mind is full
my body is settled
my breath is soft.

Awareness comes to mind
dwelling in stillness
contemplating sounds of nature
contact with the earth.

My mind is alive, alert, empty
enjoying a freedom
sitting without wanting.

Content in the moment
within a quiet sanctuary
that is full of joy.

Awakening to the glorious
realisation of this
precious life.

Resting

Rest here for a while
my pretty one
linger and lay yourself down.

Sink into the serenity of silence
drifting back and forth
in the emptiness of time.

No frame, no strain to tempt
you away from this moment
of stillness deepening with
every breath.

You are quiet, settled and content
to let yourself float into
an open sanctuary of awakening
in every corner of your mind.

Sinking yet rising
surrounded by light
welcoming the essence of an Angel
into the night.

This is your place
to melt and surrender
only intention awaits
oneness shining forever.

My View

When the sun shines
the valley is clear
opening its arms
to invite me in.

Mesmerising mountains
loom in the distance
monumental trees
spread across the slopes.

Terracotta earth
ripples along the plane
mixing and weaving
as far as the eye can see.

This commanding place
full of visual degree
is my valley, my view.

My awakening of a passion
deep from within
of mother, of daughter,
of woman so true.

A Gift for You

In our daily lives we experience chaos, turmoil and strife.
We seek peace, love, happiness and success. Most of the
time it is difficult to switch-off from our chattering mind.

Life is only available in the present moment, and we all have
the capacity to touch life in the here and now. We must pull
ourselves back into the present and reclaim our freedom.
We can change our habits by learning to rest in awareness
of the present, allowing our thoughts and feelings to drift in
without dwelling on them and then simply allowing them to
drift away, like clouds passing in the sky.

Practice enables us to grow increasingly more peaceful as we
choose the vibration of calm over the vibration of conflict.

You can practice sitting in the here and now with your breath,
by following my Moon to Heart Meditation.

I do hope you enjoy.

Moon to Heart Meditation

Rest in a comfortable position and close your eyes.
Look deeply into the dark space behind your closed eyes.

Look deeper and deeper into the dark cosmos gradually
Growing stronger in front of your closed eyes.

Now paint a picture of planet earth in the centre of the
    cosmos
Add into this image the full moon, brightly shining down to
    earth.

Now connect to your breath and imagine yourself floating
Above planet earth and up to the moon.

As you inhale draw the energy from the moon into your heart
As you exhale take the energy from your heart into the earth.

Inhale from the earth to your heart
Exhale from your heart to the moon
Inhale from the moon to your heart
Exhale from your heart to the earth

Repeat the last four lines for five more minutes.

Slowly bring your awareness back to your surroundings
And when you are ready gradually open your eyes.

Sit for a moment and notice how you feel

Namaste...

About the Author

Annie Moore is a Surrey (UK) based Mindful
Yoga and Meditation coach.

Annie blends her visions of nurture and nature
with her spiritual journey of wisdom and
guidance.

Her wish is to offer a means of healing through poetry,
reaching out to people who embrace their life to the full or to
those who struggle with real life pressing problems.

She receives her spiritual thoughts through contemplation
and meditation, creating visualisations and dreams to
enhance abundance and harmony.

Her inspiration is drawn from the nourishing, rich power of our
beautiful planet and from the natural surroundings where she
lives between UK and Portugal.

Annie has over twenty-five years' experience, in the wellbeing
industry linked to alternative therapies, energy work and
mindfulness.

Her heart and soul are deeply rooted in guiding her clients
on a journey of healing and transformation so they can
create a better more positive life filled with love, happiness,
and peace.

Thank You

To my dear wonderfully talented and supportive friend Kate for her beautiful illustrations that light up the pages of this book.

Thank you to my dear husband Terry and family for supporting me and giving me the strength to believe in myself.

Thank you to Tony for his honest, helpful advice.

To all my wonderful social media community, who have shared and liked what I have written.

To my fabulous book designer Annette who has miraculously transformed my poems into a beautiful legible book.